The Nature Kid's Guide to
ANTEATERS

DAVID ANDERSON

LP Media Inc. Publishing
Text copyright © 2026 by LP Media Inc.

For information address LP Media Inc. Publishing,
30012 Variolite St NW, Princeton MN 55371
www.lpmedia.org

Publication Data

Anteaters
The Nature Kid's Guide to Anteaters — First edition.

Summary: "Learn all about Anteaters, the Nature Kid Way"
— Provided by publisher.

ISBN: 979-8-89818-262-5

[1. Anteaters – Non-Fiction] I. Title.

Title: The Nature Kid's Guide to Anteaters

CONTENTS

NO TEETH NEEDED

Slurp! An anteater swallows hundreds of ants without chewing.

Most animals need teeth to survive. Not the anteater!

This amazing creature has zero teeth and does not need a single one. Every day it eats thousands of ants and termites, swallowing them whole without ever chewing.

The real work happens inside. A powerful stomach crushes the insects into tiny pieces. Small bits of sand and grit the anteater swallows on purpose help grind things up even more.

No teeth, no problem. The anteater has a system — and it works perfectly.

EXTREME BODIES

A giant anteater stretches about 7 feet from nose to tail — longer than most adult humans are tall!

Swoosh! A long, furry tail drags across the dusty ground.

Anteaters look like no other animal. They have a long snout shaped like a tube. Their tiny mouth is only as wide as a pencil tip — just big enough for a tongue to slip through.

Some anteaters are as big as a large dog. Others are as small as a squirrel. But all of them have strong front legs and long tails.

Thick fur covers their body, and their ears are small and round. Every part of an anteater is built for one thing: finding bugs.

An anteater visits up to 200 ant and termite nests every single day!

Scratch! An anteater tears open a termite mound for a quick meal.

Anteaters are smart about how they eat. They only snack at each ant hill for a few minutes, then move on to the next one.

Why leave so fast? If they ate all the ants, there would be none left. By eating just a little, the **colony** can grow back. The anteater can return for another meal later.

Even within a colony, anteaters pick carefully. They go for the smaller worker ants and avoid the large soldier ants, whose powerful bites can hurt even through the anteater's tough skin.

DEADLY DIGGERS

10

Stretch! A giant anteater stands up and stretches its sharp claws.

Anteaters may look gentle, but they can be fierce. When a **predator** gets too close, watch out! An anteater stands up tall on its back legs.

Then it swipes with its long, sharp claws. These claws can hurt even a jaguar or a puma. Most predators quickly learn to stay away.

An anteater fights only to stay safe. It would rather walk away from trouble. But if it has to fight, it is ready. Giant anteaters have even killed big cats that attacked them.

WANDERING WORLDS

Rustle! A giant anteater walks through the open plains.

Anteaters live in Central and South America. Some roam grassy plains. Others live deep in thick rain forests.

Each species likes a different home. Giant anteaters walk across wide open fields and savannas. Smaller species like the tamandua and the tiny silky anteater spend most of their lives up in the trees, using their tails to grip branches and rarely touching the ground.

Wherever they live, anteaters need lots of ants and termites nearby. A good home means plenty of food to find every single day.

TONGUE TWISTERS

Flick! An anteater's sticky tongue zaps in and out super fast.

An anteater's tongue is amazing. A giant anteater's tongue can be 2 feet long! That is longer than your arm.

The tongue flicks in and out up to 150 times every minute. Sticky spit coats the tongue, and ants and termites get stuck on it like glue. Each flick catches dozens of bugs.

The tongue is thin and round, like a piece of spaghetti. It reaches deep inside ant nests to grab the bugs hiding in the darkest tunnels.

An anteater's tongue starts way back at its chest bone, not its mouth!

GIANT WONDERS

16

Thump! A giant anteater plods along the grassy savanna.

The giant anteater is the biggest of all anteaters. It can weigh about 90 pounds — as heavy as a large dog. Its long, bushy tail trails behind it like a flag.

Giant anteaters live on the ground. They roam open grasslands looking for food all day. At night, they curl up and use their bushy tail like a warm blanket.

These animals walk alone most of the time. A giant anteater is quiet and shy, but it covers miles of ground each day searching for its next meal.

SILKY
SECRETS
FUN FACT!
Silky anteaters can hang from branches by their tail while eating — like a furry acrobat!
18

Look! A tiny golden silky anteater crawls along in the treetops.

The silky anteater is the smallest anteater in the world. It weighs only about 8 ounces — less than a can of soup! Its soft, golden fur looks like cotton.

Silky anteaters live in trees. They come out at night to find ants and sleep curled up on a branch during the day.

Their fur blends in with the fluffy seed pods on silk cotton trees. This clever camouflage helps them hide from hungry birds and snakes.

TAMANDUA TRAVELS

Crunch! A northern tamandua rips into a tree branch full of ants.

The northern tamandua lives in Mexico and Central America. It is a medium-sized anteater, about the size of a house cat. It likes warm forests with many trees.

This anteater spends time on the ground and in trees. Its **prehensile** tail grips branches like an extra hand, helping it climb slowly but safely.

Northern tamanduas eat ants and termites found in trees. They use their sharp claws to open up bark and find the food hiding inside.

Northern tamanduas sleep curled up in hollow trees during the day, then hunt all night!

SOUTHERN SURVIVORS

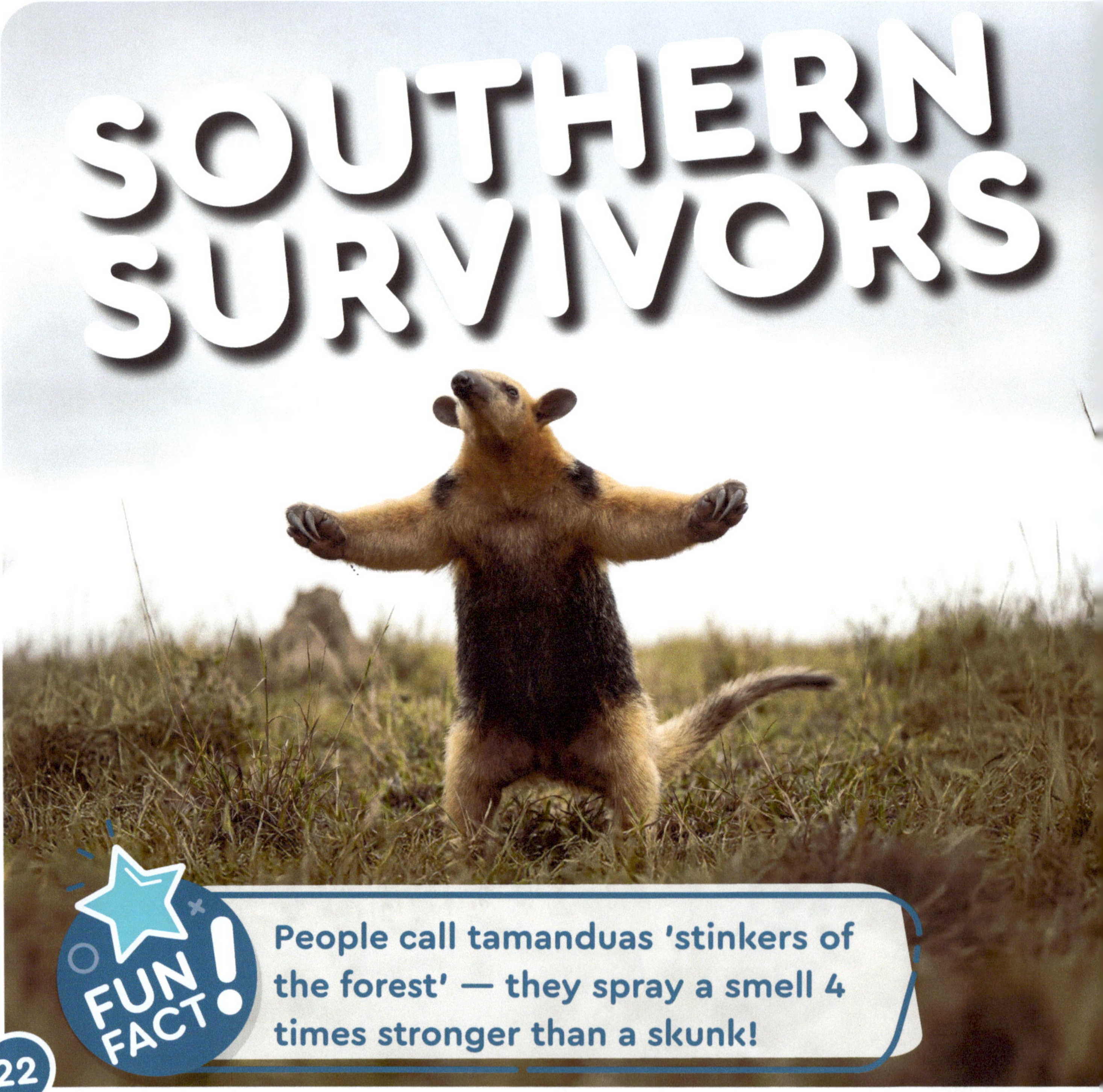

FUN FACT!

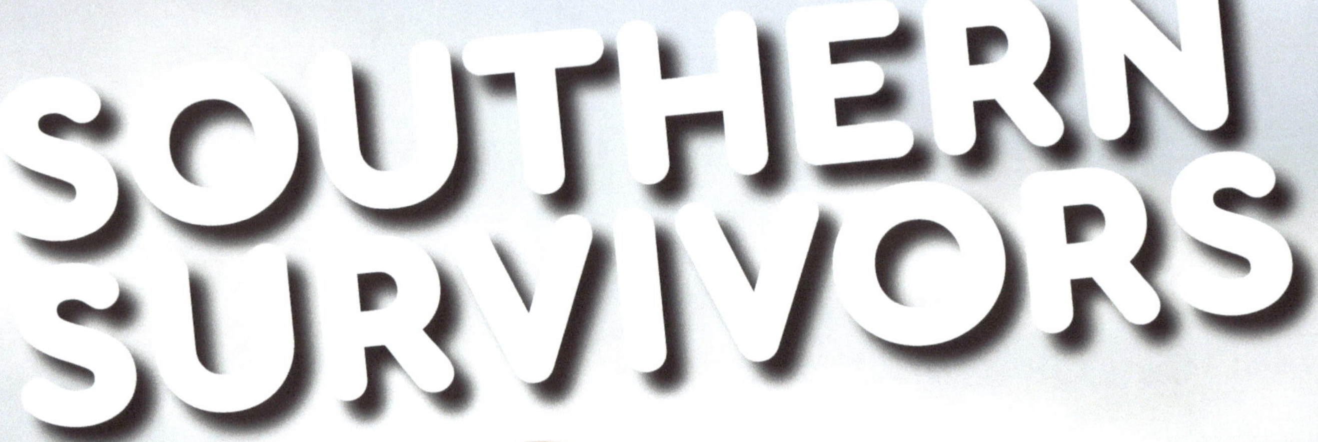

People call tamanduas 'stinkers of the forest' — they spray a smell 4 times stronger than a skunk!

Hiss! A southern tamandua puffs up to scare off a hawk.

The southern tamandua lives in South America. It can be found in forests, grasslands, and even near rivers. It looks a lot like its northern cousin.

Southern tamanduas have a special marking. A dark patch shaped like a vest covers their back and sides. This bold pattern makes them easy to spot.

When scared, a southern tamandua stands up and spreads its arms wide. It tries to look as big and scary as it can. This trick often sends predators running the other way.

CLAW CHAMPIONS

Riiip! Powerful claws tear through a rock-hard termite mound.

Anteaters have some of the strongest claws in the animal world. Their front claws are long and curved, perfect for ripping open ant and termite mounds.

These mounds can be as hard as concrete. But an anteater digs right through them in seconds. Nothing stops those powerful claws.

To keep their claws sharp, anteaters walk on their knuckles. They tuck the claws under their feet with every step. Sharp claws mean easy meals.

SUPER SNIFFERS

Sniff, sniff! An anteater's long nose follows a trail of ants.

An anteater's nose is truly special. It can smell ants and termites hiding underground! Its sense of smell is 40 times better than a human's.

The long snout works like a hose. Air flows in through two tiny holes at the tip, and the smells zoom up to the brain in a flash.

Anteaters do not have good eyesight. They cannot see well at all. But they do not need to — their super nose finds all the food they need.

An anteater sniffs nonstop while it walks, checking every single step for hidden food!

PIGGYBACK PUPS

A baby giant anteater rides on its mom's back for almost a whole year!

Whomp! A baby anteater rides right on top of its mother's back.

Mother anteaters carry their babies on their backs. A baby holds on tight to its mother's thick fur, clinging on as she walks and digs for food.

An anteater has only one baby at a time. The baby looks just like a small copy of its mom. Its fur pattern blends right in, keeping it hidden from predators.

As the baby grows, it starts to explore. It slides off and tests its own claws. Soon it will find its own ants to eat and start life on its own.

TONGUE TWINS

A pangolin's sticky tongue can stretch over 16 inches — longer than its own body!

Zap! A pangolin flicks its long, sticky tongue, just like an anteater.

Anteaters are not the only animals that eat ants this way. Pangolins in Africa and Asia use long, sticky tongues too. So do echidnas in Australia.

These animals are not related to anteaters at all. They just found the same answer to the same problem. Scientists call this **convergent evolution**.

Aardvarks in Africa eat ants too. They also have long snouts and big claws. Nature came up with the same brilliant idea in many different places around the world!

ANTEATER ALLIES

Click! A camera snaps a photo of an anteater crossing a road.

People and anteaters share the land in many places. In some towns, anteaters wander through yards at night. People have learned to live with these unusual neighbors.

Anteaters help people by eating pests. Ants and termites can damage homes and crops. By snacking on them, anteaters keep the numbers down.

Some people in South America see anteaters as special. They tell old stories about them, and anteaters are part of their history and culture.

NIGHT SHIFT

A giant anteater uses its bushy tail as a blanket — wrapping it over its whole body to stay warm while it sleeps!

34

Sniff! A giant anteater moves through the dark, nose low to the ground.

Most giant anteaters are most active in the late afternoon and evening, when the air is cooler and the savanna is quiet. When they live near people, they shift fully to nighttime to stay out of sight.

When it is time to rest, an anteater finds a secluded spot and curls up on the ground. Its long bushy tail folds over its body like a blanket, keeping it warm through the night.

Unlike most animals, anteaters have no fixed home. Every night, they find a new spot and settle in wherever feels safe.

ROADSIDE RESCUE

Swerve! A truck passes an anteater walking on the road.

Anteaters face many dangers from people. Busy roads cut through their **habitat**, and many anteaters are hit by cars and trucks each year.

Ranches and farms also take up land where anteaters used to roam. Fires set to clear land can hurt them too. Their homes are shrinking fast.

But people are working to help. Some groups build safe paths under roads for anteaters to cross. Others protect large areas of wild land. With help, anteaters can have room to live and thrive.

SPOT ONE!

The San Diego Zoo has kept giant anteaters since 1932 — making it one of the longest running anteater exhibits in the world!

Wow! A giant anteater shuffles through its pen at the zoo.

Most kids in the US will never walk through a South American savanna. But that does not mean you cannot meet a real anteater up close.

Many zoos across North America keep giant anteaters, and some also have tamanduas and silky anteaters. These animals are active and fascinating to watch, especially around feeding time when their long tongues get to work.

Look up your nearest zoo before you visit to see if they have anteaters. Some zoos also have keeper talks where you can learn even more.

GLOSSARY

colony

A large group of insects that live and work together.

predator

An animal that hunts other animals for food.

habitat

The natural place where an animal lives.

prehensile

Able to grip and hold things, like a monkey's tail.

convergent evolution

When different animals develop similar features on their own.

www.ingramcontent.com/pod-product-compliance
Lightning Source LLC
Chambersburg PA
CBHW041608110726
48005CB00002B/336